The Eye of a Fisherman

A Fisherman's Life on the Water and Beyond

A lifelong fisherman and world traveler shares a few of his angling experiences and other adventures, along with some memorable observations about life beyond the abundant waters.

Rich Robinson

AuthorHouse™
1663 Liberty Drive
Bloomington, IN 47403
www.authorhouse.com
Phone: 833-262-8899

Because of the dynamic nature of the Internet, any web addresses or links contained in this book may have changed since publication and may no longer be valid. The views expressed in this work are solely those of the author and do not necessarily reflect the views of the publisher, and the publisher hereby disclaims any responsibility for them.

Any people depicted in stock imagery provided by Getty Images are models, and such images are being used for illustrative purposes only. Certain stock imagery © Getty Images.

This book is printed on acid-free paper.

ISBN: 979-8-8230-3613-9 (sc)
ISBN: 979-8-8230-3614-6 (hc)
ISBN: 979-8-8230-3615-3 (e)

Library of Congress Control Number: 2024922170

Print information available on the last page.

Published by AuthorHouse 12/04/2024

authorHOUSE®

"Mother, mother ocean, I have heard your call…and in your belly you hold the treasure that few have seen, most of them dreams."

--From "A Pirate Looks at 40" by Jimmy Buffett

**RIP, J.B. You helped me want to be a maverick (and a pirate). I'm still trying.

Dedication

For Mary, who encouraged my love of fishing and was a very capable fisherwoman in her own right.

And to Mary, who was also my travel companion and who shared my love of adventure and curiosity about the wonders of nature.

The author's late wife Mary

Contents

Part II: Other Awesome Adventures and Special Observations

Acknowledgments

With great appreciation to David Robinson, an accomplished author, for his able guidance and assistance and to his artist wife, Lynn, for her incredible creativity in directing the art. And to every companion who has shared in my piscatorial adventures and helped celebrate my rewarding life on or near water. And finally, to my Dad, who started it all.

An Angler Remembers

In retrospect, my time pursuing fish has become less about fishing and more about finding a reflective state of mind—a place to be "re-nurtured." I have been blessed with a great sense of appreciation for our natural state. I have also been graciously given amazing opportunities to find joy and AWE in being with friends who share in the joy of the hunt, not necessarily the catch. It's the road, not the destination.

Webster's Dictionary explains that to be in awe is "to have a mixed feeling of reverence, fear, and wonder, caused by something majestic. Reverence is applied to a feeling of deep respect, mingled with love for something one holds sacred."

And, so too, have I learned that most of my memorable piscatorial adventures have often been when the creel and fish box have ended up empty. When one must acknowledge that someone with a far greater gift than the ones we mere mortals have has painted a canvas to illustrate an event or experience that simply can't be described. When the impact of the experience is so magical that it surpasses the joy of feeling the tug at the end of one's fishing line. Those times when one is mesmerized by the sound of a river rushing through a stand of pines at sunset or seeing a Manta Ray's aerial ballet or a giant bluefin tuna going airborne in pursuit of its meal. Also, there are times when the fish box is full, and we share tequila shots with friends as we return to port with a following sea. Those are the times that make magical memories.

This little book, then, is a collection of snippets, places, and events that are important to me—events that I cherish. While I hope you get something from its content, I wrote this more for myself as a way to acknowledge the awe of nature, her waters, and its contents. Also, to say my thanks to the many who have touched and influenced my life and its often-haphazard trajectory. You know who you are, and you are loved.

I

PART

A Poetic Recall of Fishing Adventures

Counting Critters

Log from the Sea of Cortez
Steinbeck and Ricketts were counters
of nudibranchs and urchins
now kept in jars
at Monterey's Aquarium.
What a thrill it would have been to share their adventures,
and a few beers.

Baja's Sea Circus

Whale sharks and porpoises,
Pargos and Porgys
acrobatic mantas
a leaping ballet with
an audience of sea birds and shore birds,
you, too, if you're lucky,
admission is free
no returns.

Spanish Lesson

Que Honda Pangueros
Hay Jurel?
Si, amigo, there are yellowtail,
La agua esta tranquilo?
Si senor, the water is calm.
Hay Cerveza frio tambien?
Si senor, there is also cold beer,
todo es bien!
Vamanos--
choose only one
Pescado o cerveza?
a difficult choice and
Not fair!

Colors

Dodos and Hoos,
opahs and boneheads,
skippys, tailers, finners, and macks,
blues, yellows, and greens,
silvers and gold,
rainbow-striped tattoos
on Marlin and Dorado,
lighting up
perfect hues
colors more intense underwater,
quick to fade, but
a palette to remember.
Cook 'em three ways—
garlic butter, Veracruz, and fried,
enough for the staff, too.

Playa Publica (Public Beach)

A beach motel with no rooms,
sleeping bags on sand,
diving pelicans
a wake-up call.
The first beer
clears my head,
loving the Baja sun.
Maybe catch a fish today,
maybe not, but
todo es bien (*all is well*).
A mega hotel with mega toys
now covers that once special beach,
It was called Nopolo.
The beach was better

Islas

Islas Carmen + Espiritu Santu
slept on both with Mary alone
Protecting the peninsula and
the critters of Mexico's secret sea,
grouper and calico below.
Cordon and Ocotillo adorn the islands above.
At night on uninhabited Carmen,
the lights of Loreto
twinkle like the stars and satellites
we watched overhead.
The Sea of Cortez
is not restless tonight,
at peace
as are we.

Buzz, The Rodfather

An introduction to Alaska
A long-lasting and permanent friendship.
I get two steelhead in 20 minutes,
Buzz gets nada, zippo, none.
I get relegated to the bow.
Alone with my Bushmills and bragging rights.
A Cowlitz River gift,
another memory
Thanks, Buzz.

Highway 1

Tijuana to Cabo—1,050 miles
on washboard roads,
way back then,
boojum and Cordons
ocotillos and mesquite,
elephant trees and palo verde,
all make shade
when the Baja sun is high
azure seas & crimson sunsets,
beaches covered with bleached bones
A history of once colorful sea-going critters,
now a tapestry of white.
But the Sea of Cortez
is still blue and beautiful.

Fisherpersons Speak

Bait sticks and bimini twists (fish knot)
"Keep moving right, guys!"
"Biter on the stern!"
"Get a fresh bait, fellas."
"Hook up!"
"I've got color."
"I need a gaff."
"And a camera."
"And a beer!"

Campo San Nicholas

A long-gone gathering place for fishing friends,
yellowtail for the taking,
memories for the making,
and beer for the drinking,
RIP Antonio and Gilberto.
and Ozwaldo and Alfredo before you,
You all checked out early,
Salud, amigos,
anchors up and safe passage.

Baja Mornings

Something about Baja's warm pre-dawn winds,
phosphorescence on the water,
heading to Punto Lobo
with someone loved,
fish don't matter now,
First yellowtail brings her to her knees,
Love that warm wind,
loved that lady.

Something About Salmon

There's something about
kings or chinooks,
silvers or cohos,
pinks or humpies,
chums or dogs,
sockeyes or reds,
how they live,
how they fight,
how they die,
how they are remembered,
how they taste.

First Steelhead

A winter drift in January,
on the Skykomish,
naked Alder and Aspen
on barren banks,
a thousand shades of grey,
steel-colored water,
holding steel-colored fish,
elusive metallic fish,
boated one,
released one,
first steelhead,
another gift from Buzz—

Remembering Howard

I wish I could have known you better,
Who could not love you?
from a trauma doc in Vietnam
to a fishing friend,
cigars at dusk,
brandy in hand,
Campo San Nicholas too,
Barbless hooks,
you a sportsman
and my hero.
I miss you, Howard
See you on the other side.

Living Turtles

Turtle corrals at Gonzaga Bay
Between papa Fernandez's and Alfonsinas,
abandoned now thankfully,
Wicked west winds there meant
kite flying, not fish frying.
The view is a bonus,
turtles now thrive.
The Bay still inviting.

Chinook

You reeled me in,
a promise of starboard silver
Some crazy, chrome-colored plug
Imitating a wounded herring,
King on!
wanting freedom,
wish granted,
gift of a parted line,
Then you became a geriatric marathoner,
with mottled skin and a hooked jaw,
libido is gone, but you did your job
Going home now, big fella
Well done.
A life well-lived,
eagles prepare to feast on a parting gift.

Release Me

First light warmth,
skies on fire,
anticipation without expectation,
A sensual atmosphere,
no fish necessary,
The prize,
like a carousel's brass ring
was the catching,
not the keeping,
Heroes leave them
for manana
Fish photos are great,
and fish freedom is priceless.

Getting There Then

Tijuana to Cabo via La Paz,
Mexicana and Aeromexico,
Aero Servicos with DC-3s or 6s,
thatched hut airport,
dirt runways,
Pamilla, Hotel Cabo San Lucas, and Twin Dolphin,
Fly over the hotels
maybe someone will come,
they always do
Bienvenidos a Baja.
Making memories.

Baja Before

Before paved streets replaced dirt and dust,
The Giggling Marlin
was the place to be,
The Mar de Cortez,
rooms $23 a night
no views, no room service, no noise
brown skin on white sheets,
Before the neon and pavement of Cabo,
the cannery then, a cruise ship terminal now,
open vistas of gulf water, then,
hotel facades now,
A few angler-explorers then,
a flotilla of wealth now,
Generator lights off at 10 p.m.,
Darkness, peace and quiet then,
all night noise and bright lights now
a special place then,
with special memories
Gracias, Maria,
Take me back to then.

Baja Pajaros (Birds)

Pelicanos and boobies,
shearwaters and skimmers
gannets and frigate birds,
follow the pajaros
some, like flying dinosaurs,
frigate birds on the sea surface,
guaranteed big fish beneath
God's best fishing guides for free,
amigos del mar.

For Alano

Introduced you to Baja,
your first fish,
you were hooked
smiling at a marlin's freedom,
tuna too,
summer sweat
never to forget
celebrating with a six a.m. cerveza and
tequila shots at day's end,
loving the experience
let's do it again.
Your ashes on the water
I am the lucky one,
But we both have the memories,
hasta, amigo mio.

The Joy

The pure joy of fishing
is best remembered
with friends,
it's the banter,
the beer,
and don't forget
the bragging rights
who caught what,
who sat on his butt,
Old memories
are more treasured,
and valuable
than recent dreams.
Bait sticks and bimini twists,
bloody decks and bait balls
fish speak--
fisherpeople understand.

Grandson's First Marlin

On his feet
Striped marlin leaping
grinding away,
leader appears,
a photo taken,
toothful grin,
freedom for the fish.
Seth, you own it,
the fish and bragging rights,
the marlin got bigger,
a lesson learned,
good job,
Pepsi for you,
cerveza for me,
Well done, lad!

Pacific Northwest

In a drift boat,
freezing cold on the Skykomish,
or Humptulips or Cowlitz, Quinault, or Hoh,
Ancestral waters,
holding ancestral fish,
but when nary a fish is boated,
with friends
Pass the whisky,
just for warmth,
a memory made to be enjoyed
on another warm day.

Amigos

Punta Colorado on the sea wall,
with Chuck, Mike, and Damon,
Alan and Johnny,
Pacificos and bragging rights,
Sometimes storms and winds,
so, no fishing,
What, no fish?
On a calm sea,
lines out,
no biters
joy in the moment.
Islands teeming with birds and cacti,
sun and shadows make a quilt,
everything is a gift,
nothing taken for granted.
In the past, fish counts were important,
a measure of a good day on the water,
now it's great to just be on the water.
memories that never fade

Vultures on Cacti

Turkey vultures perched
like totems
on Cordon cacti,
waiting for the sun
with wings spread
to go aloft,
searching for carrion and clouds.
Your views of the aquamarine Sea of Cortez
Worth it all
take my spirit aloft.

Records

If I was counting…
a 206-pound Bluefin,
101-pound Big Eye,
89-pound yellowfin,
68-pound wahoo,
too many marlin, yellowtail, and dorados to count,
no records for certain,
meals, stories, and memories,
but who's counting

Escape Plan

When I get pissed off
about our government,
the economy and a
claustrophobic climate,
I heal with thoughts of
calm seas and warm Baja winds,
The best therapy.

Isla La Guardia

Protects Bahia de Los Angeles,
home to whale sharks,
behemoths casting shadows on the sea floor,
tolerating curious tourists,
El Refugio to the north
the best Baja anchorage
but wicked north winds
can pummel a 24 foot Skipjack,
extinguishing my cigar,
divine guidance shows the way
to the bar.

Highway 1, Again

It's the early '70s,
turning left at Guerro Negro,
past Vizcaino
San Ignacio's lagoon waits,
date palms and cold Tecates.
The mission has stood since 1697,
It makes me feel old.

Islas #2

Marine monoliths,
home to Cordon cactus
rattlesnakes without rattles,
eons of white bird guano
protectors of bays and beaches,
and memories of erotic encounters,
in tepid waters,
forever memories.

Sea Pirates

Mother Ocean
There's no reason for plundering,
Thieves stealing your precious bounty
more than they can eat,
deserving less than they want.
It takes more than a village
to save our planet.
Our oceans and their critters
are our lifeline,
our future.
Our mandate is to protect her.

38

San Quintin

Holding bleached sand dollars
El Molino Viejo
howling winds,
maritime ghosts
hiding and hoping amidst the dunes.
Big clams too
at testiculos level,
hold your breath.

On Tackle

Tadys and Salas,
flat falls and phooeys,
jigmasters and senators,
bone jigs and red yarn hooks,
Before spectra and
two-speeds,
fish had a better chance.
Some memories like
rusted hooks and sunbaked lines,
are useless,
others, like treasured reels and Sage rods,
are kept with one's most valued possessions.

Leftovers

A quorum of carnivores,
a carrion eaters convention,
eagles and ravens converge
on the remnants of river warriors
leaving a cemetery of bones.
Salmon warriors.

Paralelo 28

The monument divides Norte & Sur,
the resident osprey,
a desert guardian
sits on the monument,
with her nest,
year after year.
Bienvenidos, Amigos.

Guerro Negro

Black warrior,
salt works and wind,
turn left to azure seas
via San Ignacio,
a desert oasis,
with date palms and brackish water
and cold beer.

Saving the Vaquita

Why kill the tiny threatened vaquita
when hunting tortuva for their bladders,
to cure Asian prostate problems and pecker itch?
How about an educational suppository
for your brain?
So few remain,
it's love and protection they deserve.

Pilot Bob

Bob flew beavers
to the shallow stream at Rancho Meling
ponds for trout
elusive rainbows still hiding
under the pines.
Lucky few to witness
great job, beavers.
Are the trout still there?
Maybe.
Gracias Roberto.

Me Gusto Loreto (I like Loreto)

Like riding on a rainbow,
the view of the sea
is it blue or green?
something in between?
past Santa Rosalia
where an Eiffel-designed "church in a kit"
got on the wrong boat,
built by locals
it stands today,
past Mulege, home of date groves
and Hotel Serenidad,
a pig roast and margaritas every Saturday,
Loreto, you kept your charm,
Your current mission, built in 1744,
is 200 years older than I am,
it still welcomes the devout,
and me,
your malecon, too, welcomes young lovers, fat cruise folks,
and me,
Stay as you are, por favor.

Ode to Ray Canon

The "Sea of Cortez" was our Baja bible,
an early invitation to know the majesty of Baja,
an early invitation to fish in virgin waters,
an early invitation to a peninsula like no other.
I wish you could have kept her as she was,
you gave me an early invitation to awe,
I RSVP'd 100 times,
no regrets,
we shared her at her best
Muy gracias, Senor Canon.

Isla Cedros

A third-world island with
first-class fishing,
for amigos Dan, Jeff, Mike, Stan, Russ, Johnny, Damon, and me,
Yellowtail and calico bass abound,
A repository for Guerro Negro's salt
headed to the Orient
in the shadow of the massive transport ships,
"Got to stop wishin',
got to go fishin'
down to rock bottom,"
where fat sheepshead and grouper
are waiting,
and don't forget those husky yellowtail.

Thanks to Baja's Early Hoteliers

You came early before the congestion,
before dense development,
we owe you, boys:
Tabor's Flying Sportsman,
Walter's Buena Vista, Parr's Hacienda,
Van Warmer's Palmas Cortez, Playa del Sol, Punta Colorado (RIP),
Johnson's Serenidad in Mulege,
Ida Meling's Ranch and Mike's Sky Place,
homesteading before Highway 1
great fishing places,
long gone fishing faces,
Thank you all.

Flossing Fish

Sockeye salmon
heading to Lake Illiama,
nose to tail,
mouths agape,
not wanting to be flossed by a fly,
tossed by some hopeful angler,
most make it to the lake,
deservedly
a few to the grill.

Baja Chaos

A thousand leaping porpoises,
a bazillion bait fish,
whose scales turn the water silver,
gannets, pelicans, and boobies
dive to get their share,
seals join in,
who knows what lurks beneath,
it's show time in the Sea of Cortez

Awesome Authors

Zane, Ernest, Roderick, Holder, and Heilner,
you put your memories in print.
Memories of pioneering efforts,
to subdue monster fish,
with pretty primitive tackle,
fueling a young boy's fishing fantasies,
as did my father.

Midriff Mothership

At first sight
a scary scow
we look for skull and crossbones,
once a tug or shrimp boat,
now a rusted floating hotel,
plugged with fisher folk,
pangas in tow,
moving at night
through the Midriff Islands
of the Sea of Cortez,
angling competitors at dawn,
best buds with beer at night,
Damon, Johnny, Alan, Mike, Stan and me,
laughing and loving
the experience,
now another memory,
with an unlikely chance
of making more.

Damon, Sage, and the Kids

I pass on my Dad's fishing lessons,
a gift to son Damon
with hopes that grandsons Seth and Walker
might also appreciate those gifts.
Damon, now an able teacher
and very capable of gifting Grandson Walker,
himself not yet able or wanting to hold a rod.
And nephew Sage, an accomplished fisherman,
rod builder and friend, a teacher too.
We have shared the joy of being on the water
with or without fish,
for the table.
And we have laughed and made memories.
I hope that Damon, Sage, Seth, and Walker
will continue and remember where it
all began,
as I do.

Take a Kid Fishing

A kid with a stick, a hook, and a worm.
First bluegill could mean an angler in the making.
Maybe a dad, brother, or friend provides a spark
leading to a closet full of tackle,
a future of travel to faraway places,
maybe big fish bragging rights,
wonderful memories,
and a mountain of credit card debt.

Touching Tarpon

Florida Keys stop off in Islamorada
Robbie's Place
A Bloody Mary and front-row seat,
Giant Tarpon, like airborne silver submarines
snatch baitfish from the hands of startled tourists,
eighty or ninety pounds of acrobatic energy,
such fun to witness.

Author's son and grandson in Loreto, Baja

Author's grandson with his
first Dorado (Mahi-mahi)

The author and Mary with limits
in Prince Rupert, Canada

II

PARarT

Other Awesome Adventures and Special Observations

Author and Mary in Baja
California, Mexico

There is no end to life's experiences. So much more than time spent on the water. This exercise in reliving other awesome adventures and memories has been therapeutic for me, as I am getting a little longer in the tooth. Memories are becoming more important. They are often pleasant distractions, helping me cope with the loss of my partner of 30+ years.

Buried in Normandy

During a trip to France, we had an opportunity to visit The Le Combe Cemetery near the Normandy Coast. It was hard for me to understand and justify the burial of German soldiers in France. The Le Combe Cemetery alone holds the bodies and souls of 21,222 warriors who died fighting in WW II. The families of most of the U.S. soldiers were given the option of repatriation to the U.S. or burial in France. Three-fourths of the American soldiers came home. It appears that the German soldiers filled their places.

The headstones of those elite bastards who were part of the killing machine known as the "SS" had their designations removed from the headstones by grinding. That's because French citizens and many others would urinate on the grave markers. Six million Jews would stand in line with me if they could.

We also stopped at the American cemetery adjacent to Omaha Beach and the English Channel. We were moved—as most anyone would be—by the sobering sight of 9,389 headstones. A bugler plays taps as our flag is lowered at sundown. We and the other visitors bow our heads. Tears are shed freely.

It was a glaring reminder of the ultimate sacrifice made for our freedom. The human cost of war is so evident on the coast of Normandy. Look hard, and you can almost see the blood of the fallen, many in their teens, while families and friends waited for their return, which would never happen.

The Dangerous Summer

If you are not a Hemingway fan or reader or do not care about bullfighting, the name Antonio Ordonez would not be familiar. But, for those of us who have read Papa' H's accounts of the fights and know of his close bond with Ordonez, who at one time was called the number one bullfighter in all of Spain, maybe the world, Ordonez is rather special. He was one of the two combatants featured in the Life Magazine article "The Dangerous Summer," a story of the mano y mano bullfighting duel between Ordonez and his brother-in-law, Luis Dominguin, in the summer of 1959. By many accounts, Hemingway was fading fast, both creatively and physically, yet he found the energy to document this somewhat historic battle. He described in detail the bullfights in corridas (arenas) throughout Spain. The story wasn't a huge success when it appeared in the three-part Life series in 1960. It was only after Hemingway died on July 2, 1961, that the series was condensed into a more readable version and eventually published in the mid-1980s.

Island Getaway

How many times have we left Southern California's chaos, taking the midweek morning ferry to the Channel Island of Catalina.? As the old song says, "26 miles across the sea, Santa Catalina waits for me." Jumping on the ferry, sipping a Bloody Mary while waiting for a glimpse of this magical refuge. It was one of our favorite getaways, but not on a weekend or in Summer, and especially not when the cruise ships have docked just outside Avalon Harbor. Only on those days when the Island is owned by those who live and work there, and folks like us seeking an open spot of sand or an uncluttered view of the vintage casino (gathering place, not the gambling kind). Those times when one can smell the eucalyptus and appreciate the din of woodpeckers and gulls while admiring the homes of the affluent and watching boats of all sizes bob up and down in the harbor. Those times when we would mix with the locals at the Marlin Club and dine on monkey balls (ahi tuna) at the lobster trap restaurant next door. There were so many times that a loving couple found enchantment at the old Zane Grey Pueblo, a venue where love was made, and books were written about cowboys and fishing for giant swordfish and tuna, all while seeing the lights of the mainland 26 miles away. There were also many times we entered the chilly water off Pebbly Beach to snorkel amid schools of orange Garibaldis and calico bass. And how many times did we walk the empty streets of Avalon at night, hearing only the sound of waves lapping against the sea wall?

And how many times have we shared our Catalina dream with close friends, drinking and dining and playing miniature golf for more drinks before heading to Big Olafs (gone, but not forgotten) for ice cream? Alas, there were many times, but still not enough. The future is here, and the past is just a joyful memory.

More on Antonio Ordonez

Ordonez died of cancer in December 1998 at the age of 66. About half of his ashes are buried where the bulls enter the corrida in Ronda, Spain. In Ronda, Hemingway's relationship with Ordonez is memorialized with statues, street names, and historical memories.

One Sunday in 1962, when I was an adventuresome 17-year-old, I saw Ordonez fight what was described as "an undistinguished bull" in the Tijuana Corrida. During the fight, one bull gored Ordonez in his inner thigh. In a state of beer-induced euphoria, I raced to the bowels of the arena to step on a remaining banderilla (short barbed lance), which pulled free. This blood-encrusted memento was one of my most prized possessions for many years.

Magical Highways

As part of my love for seeing new places, I have had the pleasure of traveling on many of our highways and byways. Like a stroll on the Yellow Brick Road, searching for answers from an undiscovered place, where joy comes from the pursuit and sometimes the place itself. The roads that surprise with views of a restless ocean or heavily scented forests. Like the road from Cooke City, Montana to Cody, Wyoming, or Highway 101 on the California Coast, or Route 66, or the road out of Jackson Hole that passes the Oxbow Bend in the Snake River, with the Teton Mountain range in the background. And don't forget Hwy 395 passing East of my magnificent Eastern High Sierras, with old Mr. Whitney as its guardian and sentinel. And then there is the road from Miami to Key West, and the one in Old Smokey National Park, and many others.

Joe is Dying

The old man has cracked Joe's door and is preparing to visit. How does one manage a 74-year-old friendship when your pal is getting ready to pass on?

It began at La Canada Junior High School (California) sometime in the 1950s. We were dealing with pimples, trying to figure out girls and our own physiology, and involved with Cub Scouts and baseball, bikes, and bubble gum. From then to now, so many ups and downs, marriages, divorces, gains and losses, tears and laughter—the stuff of passages. We shared successes and failures and tried to prop each other up when we lost our friends. Yes, we talked often. Yes, we mumbled "I love you" at the end of our phone conversations. But I never expected to feel this kind of loss. This kind of pain. This kind of love for Joe. I am going to miss you, buddy. (Will you remember the time Pete lit farts at that motel in Newport Beach? That should make you smile.) You will be joining old friends: Tom, Tony, Geoff, Shari, Marcia, Hank, and my Mary. You will be well received. Leave the light on for me.

Entertaining Otters

Those wishing to escape the urban congestion of Southern California by heading north can make an entertaining visit to the charming town of Morro Bay. Other than the obvious beauty of this oceanside village, a well-kept secret is the flotilla of otters that inhabit the bay. With pups on their tummies, they are highly visible from shore upon which they will never set foot, as they spend their entire lives on or under the sea. Feeding on clams, abalone, and mussels, our otters are indeed entertaining. Once almost obliterated for their fur, these seagoing rascals have rebounded and are a delight to watch.

My Favorite Things

Beach agates, an intricate piece of driftwood, pine cones, bird feathers, and petrified wood. (What reason does one have to keep such things?) None come close to the value of my time with you. Treasured finds, maybe, but worthless when compared to your love, and I would find a million of them to trade for your return. Or the value of such items when compared to the worth of a loving family and friends. The importance of such relationships cannot be quantified. They just give meaning to life.

Rancho dos Cuervos de Oro

You are an 82-year-old jigsaw puzzle with a few pieces missing. Additions made with no logical sense. A classic haphazard design that almost exists in a state of arrested decay. Not a true angle to be found. It was love at first sight, with an expansive 270-degree view on a 3.5-acre hilltop. With a lot of hard work and sweat, it gradually evolved into a country cabin oozing with charm. From an early nightmare with its orange, cat pee-stained carpet and green wallpaper to a cozy natural wood abode with stained glass windows and a massive rock fireplace. It is called "Rancho dos cuervos de oro" (Ranch of two golden crows), appropriate because of the hundreds of noisy crows that frequent the property. It's a welcoming and comforting place where we lived and loved together for 30 years. The panorama is spectacular, with the Coronado Islands in the distance, and beaches of Coronado City, La Jolla, and Del Mar at midrange, and the cities of Santee and Lakeside in the foreground. We gladly share our refuge with coyotes, quail, rattlesnakes, and roadrunners. Our springer spaniel pets are buried here, and someday, our cremains will be here, too, where they belong.

Bosque de Apache, New Mexico

Midway between Casa Grande and Albuquerque, New Mexico, is a wetland ecosystem renowned by birders for its waterfowl populations. Many will agree that the whooping cranes that arrive by the thousands every fall are most entertaining.

On a solo trip through this area early one September, I wasn't expecting any special wildlife encounters. However, I (and one other wandering tourist) got to witness the early arrival of these amazing birds. They land in knee-deep estuaries in order to deter predators and with a din of incredible magnitude. I was blessed with a front-row seat in one of nature's most extraordinary events. Departing for more appetizing environs at dawn, the cranes return each night to their shared and protected sanctuary. One more National Geographic documentary that I was privileged to see.

Shame on Us

History books are often woefully silent when it comes to the social criminality of our forefathers and their evil deeds committed in the name of geographical expansion or progress. How could it be that our indigenous peoples, occupants of their own lands, were slaughtered like defenseless bison or penned in claustrophobic reservations like cattle?

How could a civilized nation turn its paranoid back on the innocent victims of the Holocaust? And we, who are now inclined to stick our intrusionary noses in the civil affairs of other nations, still try to justify the internment of non waring U.S. Japanese citizens in prison-like camps? Will we ever be able to atone for the horrific acts of our forefathers?

Will we face some appropriate punishment in the future? Stand by.

Acadia

On the rugged coast of Maine, lobsters hide as the golden leaves of Autumn blanket Acadia's hiking and biking trails. As picturesque as an East Coast destination can be, one of its major attractions is Cadillac Mountain. We joined other sleepy tourists who woke early to climb the mountain in order to claim that we were the first in the U.S. to see the sunrise. We could then boast to the residents of Tulsa, Tupelo, and Tustin that they have missed something extraordinary. Being first at anything is a wonderful thing, I guess.

Remarrying Mary

Rousting me from a sound sleep on a gently swaying anchored boat, Mary said, "Put on something nice. It's Easter, and we need to see the sunrise in the Galapagos Islands." With minimal grumbling, I stumble topside. The other 16 passengers are asleep, and the ship's captain in his freshly starched whites is at the bow, where I am led, to be informed that we will be saying our marital vows for the second time.

I become teary as we are married again. I remain pleasantly shocked at Mary's creative surprise and the abundance of champagne being poured at 5:30 in the tropical morning. It is indeed Easter, and I rejoice.

Yosemite Firefalls

From Camp Curry in the 1950s and 1960s, we watched the nightly display of fiery embers pushed from the edge of Yosemite's Glacier Point. A 3,000-foot ribbon of red and orange delighted us campers in the valley below. With a backdrop of magnificent peaks and the soothing sound of the Merced River, the firefalls might be one of "The Greatest Shows on Earth." This popular attraction was stopped in 1968 because of environmental concerns.

Havana

We followed the memory of Hemingway as he pontificated about the day's fishing adventure while sitting on bar stools at La Bodeguita (for Mojitos) and La Floridita (for Daquiris). Cigars afire. He spoke of bullfights and bullshit and his love of the local fisherman who was memorialized as the Old Man (Santiago), who talked baseball with the boy.

Hemingway's boat, "Pilar," was beautiful and buoyant and made to ply the waters of Cuba and Key West. She was lovingly cared for by Georgio Fuentes and Carlos Gutierrez. Fuentes might have been Hemingway's model for Santiago, the fisherman in Old Man and the Sea. They were both captains and fishermen who endured the drunken antics of E.H.—bloodying the deck with captive fish and his own head wounds from inebriated falls. At day's end, his trophies were hung at the docks as a testimonial to his fishing talent and an oversized ego. Most likely, the locals received the fish, a precious commodity. Pilar now rests, maintained in a state of arrested decay, at his once Cuban refuge, Finca Vigia.

The Monarchs of Morelia

On a spring day just outside Morelia, I had to stop and question my state of mind as I slowly raised my large self on the back of a a horse and rode with Mary, Jeanie,and Jimmy to see some butterflies. Arriving at unique pine-covered hills, we are in awe of the millions of orange and black butterflies decorating every square inch of bark and branch. They've flown thousands of miles from the north to land in the highlands of Mexico. To see these beautiful winged creatures was an ecological gift. For us, it was just one more National Geographic moment, particularly when they all took flight as if by some silent signal.

Key West

A mere 159 miles south of Miami, past many islands and atolls with odd names like Marathon, Islamorada, Key Largo, and Cudjoe Key, is the end of the road. I spent over a year in the Key West area during the mid-1960s. A quiet, yet-to-be-discovered beach haven, it is now known for Conch fritters and Mallory Square, where you can join your fellow tourists to toast the sunsets. Before Jimmy Buffett sang about Captain Tony, and earlier Hemingway sat and drank at Sloppy Joe's, one could see the water, now obscured mainly by hotels and eateries. Duval Street is a congested 10-ring circus. The charm is long gone and now tarnished for me, but Key West will still welcome you and your wallet.

Mount Whitney

I have been very fortunate and often challenged during the 11 times I have climbed Mount Whitney, the towering elder statesman of the Eastern Sierras. At 14,505 feet, she stands apart as the tallest mountain in the lower 50, a magnificent monument of the Sierras. Viewed from the natural Western cowboy movie venue of the Alabama Hills, she anchors the spine of California's dominant mountain range. Each time I trekked to Mt. Whitney's summit, gazing down at the Owens Valley below, I felt as close to heaven as I would ever be. Once, when I was descending, I met a woman climber passing me on her way up the mountain. She was topless. I mentioned my surprise encounter to a ranger who was also ascending. His pace quickened.

Walk in Their Shoes

On a trip to Budapest, we stopped on the Danube River's eastern bank, where dozens of cast metal shoes have been placed. It's a solemn tribute to the innocents shot, killed, and dumped into the river during World War II. Some were still alive, chained to others who were dead. There are Fascist Hungarians rotting in hell for their heinous deed.

Walking around the somber shoe display, we are overcome. The tears of visitors to this stark and dark tribute add to the river's flow as we are again reminded of men's evil ways. Those shoes and those who occupied them will never be forgotten.

Mount Rainier

Mt. Rainier in Washington State is just a few feet below Whitney's altitude, but it is a much more difficult climb because of the snow and ice that accumulate year-round. It's also intimidating because of ice crevasses and the threat of avalanches, which increase as the temperature climbs. Most who make the trek do so with guides after completing a required class in self-arresting techniques, which are used if one should slip on a slope.

We hiked in groups of five and roped together with a guide. Those unable to make it to the top are left on the side of the trail with a sleeping bag, to be picked up on the return. As we plodded up with heads down, wearing crampons for traction and relying on adrenaline for progress, I wondered why I was making this climb on such a bitterly cold day. My good friend, Alan, got lucky when he was left with a very attractive lady hiker and only one sleeping bag. Sadly, he was too tired to do much more than sleep.

Amazing Africa

Our first trip to Africa in 2010 began a love affair that continues to this day. I was drawn to the continent four more times during the next ten years. We were welcomed by the ark of animals, all born free. Apex predators are always on the hunt, picking off the young and weak. Hyenas, Jackels, and vultures keep the place clean. Hemingway killed and whined when someone bagged a bigger animal, I bragged when I got a great photo.

The Serengeti Savannah is simply amazing, where the backs of Cape Buffalo and wildebeest darken the landscape. They are following the rains that grow the grasses. Nature's documentaries constantly unfolding. I have been blessed to witness. The diversity of the flora and fauna is unmatched and will not be found anywhere else in the world. While poachers threaten some species whose tusks, bones, and other anatomical assets are prized for many bizarre uses, efforts are being made to protect and save the magnificent creatures.

Each trip was a special gift.

Yellowstone

The yellow stone is sulfur. Its acrid smell adds to the magnificence of this land of mud pots and gasses. Bison cross the rivers, vapor escaping from their noses. Ignorant tourists jockey for selfies. Some get gored, others need to be. The bison and wolves are back from the edge of extinction. Ambling by aquamarine pools, these denizens of Yellowstone own it. Moose and elk also wander throughout God's zoo.

The Firehole is an appropriate name for a river in Yellowstone. At dawn, a black gnat or maybe a nymph was on my tippet. Vapors rise from the surface with the sun. A river on the rocks. Majestic mountains surround. The trees offer shade and serenity. The setting is worth much more than a trout.

Down south a bit, East of the Teton Range, the Oxbow bend in the Snake River is a place for Moose to wallow. With the Teton Range as a backdrop, it is a perfect setting for a perfect photo.

Every memory is a story. Every story spellbinding

Grand Canyon

There is no grander canyon than the vast and dramatic, intricately sculpted chasm in Northern Arizona. With a depth of more than 6,000 feet to its rock bottom, God's 2.5 billion-year-old artistic talent is on display in every season.

Our first experience seeing the Canyon up close was when we descended 6,000 feet on the Kaibab Trail. We were mesmerized by the ever-changing palette of colors, influenced by the Earth's clock and the sun's trajectory.

The Kaibab Trail leads to the Phantom Ranch, a great place to recover. Mule pack trains deliver supplies and lazy visitors, who always looked saddle sore or pleasure bent. Cold beers fix both.

It's worth repeating—there is no more spectacular canyon.

Boobs, Beads, Booze and Blues

On the few times I was on Bourbon Street in New Orleans, I was reminded of the bar scene in one of the Star Wars movies. Every imaginable critter wearing every imaginable outfit, ambling along the street, and ogling at the female tourists who bare their chests in exchange for a string of beads. It is amusing for sure, but a far cry from the historical pleasure I have received from past trips. My highlight was listening to classical music by the pioneers of blues and jazz, which came from the many clubs along this historic thoroughfare. The sounds are not always heard from a ringside seat, for the musical joy often comes from the faceless talent behind a well-used alto sax or clarinet.

Galapagos

The only time we traveled to the Galapagos islands, we were in awe of its beauty and diverse wildlife. The islands, which are a couple of clicks south of the Equator, East of Ecuador, are an ecosystem that time simply forgot. A 200-million-year-old diorama unfolds. From the Mesozoic era comes an age of modern-day dinosaurs. Marine and terrestrial iguanas are not afraid of us or the crimson Sally Lightfoot crabs that surround them. We observed blue-footed Boobies, red-throated frigate birds, and seagoing Albatross, along with Giant tortoises that get center stage. It's a cast of critters that delighted Darwin and ourselves.

Land Snakes Alive

Burmese pythons own the Everglades. Released as overgrown serpents, which were once pets, few mammals now remain, voraciously eaten. Introduced by few, now a tragedy for many, as the once diverse ecosystem is now a largely vacant bog. Man, once again, screws with Mother Nature. We wait for her revenge.

Loving Our Veterans

My license plate frame reads, "My heroes wore dog tags." I have a special place in my heart for all those who are serving or have ever served. I have been to the beaches of Normandy, the USS Arizona Memorial at Pearl Harbor, Arlington's Tomb of the Unknown Soldier, and the Vietnam Memorial in Washington, DC. I am not ashamed to say I tear up at all of them.

In the Winter of 1967, when I was discharged after a four-year stint in the Air Force, Service members, in general, were not held in high esteem. I get emotional now when seeing videos of surprise visits of our vets walking into their children's classroom or showing up to greet a spouse in an unexpected moment. Our Vets are now getting the respect that they so richly deserve. Honor flights, flyovers, and sporting event tributes during which service members are asked to stand and be recognized. There are dozens of charities supporting Vets and their families. Flags fly on Veterans and Memorial Days and every day in my front yard.

We owe everyone who wore dog tags an incredible dose of gratitude. As the saying goes, "All gave some, Some Gave All.". I am particularly supportive of the Gary Sinise Foundation and would encourage everyone to support his programs, many of which are directed at those needing unique housing because of their combat disabilities.

Cable Climbs

I only know of two exciting climbs where cables are used to assist with the steeper portions of the assent. One is Angels Landing in Zion National Park, Utah, which I did with my good friend Gary. The other is Half Dome in Yosemite National Park in California, which I climbed with friends Jack and Colleen.

The cables are there to provide psychological and physical insurance in case of a misstep. However, both hikes can still be quite intimidating, even with the cables to grip. On each climb, we came across folks who were frozen in place, scared to take another step. They could not move forward or back, which created gridlock and a significant backup of other climbers. This added tension to the already challenging environment. The fear factor has also confronted me when I have stumbled and fallen, when the consequence of a few inches would have been near fatal. The solution for such a climbing dilemma is for the obstructing climber to either recover and move on or step aside outside the cables to let the foot traffic pass.

Author and wife in Alaska

Author and Mary in Italy

The author with Mary
at Snake River Montana

The author with Mary at Normandy

The author and his wife while
wolf watching in Yellowstone

Author and Mary in Africa

Epilogue

What's Next?

Putting these thoughts together was, for me, therapeutic. Having lost my partner of 30 years to cancer just eight months ago, I have struggled to find diversions, ways to keep me from feeling bitter and sorry for myself. Mary was an integral part of so many of these adventures I have described. On many of the fishing expeditions, when she was not physically present, she was with me in spirit as she would find a way to sneak a love note somewhere in my luggage. Just as I would place similar adorations around the house or mailed by friends to spatially arrive while I was away. The point is that we loved and cared about each other and knew that we were never really apart. Now that she is gone, I feel the same way, knowing she is with me no matter where or what I am doing.

Some would say that I am getting a little long in the tooth. A metaphor that may be true, but as an octogenarian, I am blessed not only with the memory of Mary but also the ability to recall much of my past with some detail. Now, flying solo, these memories give me comfort and hope.

So, what lies ahead? My analogies go from playing in the ninth inning, with two outs and the count being three balls and two strikes, to playing in the fourth quarter, with no time-outs and two minutes to play. In both scenarios, I still have fuel in the tank. I still have things I want to accomplish, I still want to be there for others, and I still have my faith. I am just not ready to land the plane, even though I am low on fuel.

About The Author

Rich, a Southern California native, veteran, and San Diego State University graduate, retired as an administrator for the County of San Diego. His passion for fishing took him from the High Sierras lakes and streams in the 1950s to the tip of Baja California in the early 1970s, to the remote reaches of Alaska and many places in between. He remains in awe of the magnificence of the fishing experience and the wonder of nature's bounty and gifts. For more information about Rich and this book, visit richincrest@att.net

Printed in the United States
by Baker & Taylor Publisher Services